D0846966

Walking Papers

Also by Thomas Lynch

FICTION

Apparition & Late Fictions

POETRY

Skating with Heather Grace

Grimalkin & Other Poems

Still Life in Milford

NONFICTION

The Undertaking: Life Studies from the Dismal Trade

Bodies in Motion and at Rest: On Metaphor and Mortality

Booking Passage: We Irish and Americans

Walking Papers

Poems 1999–2009

THOMAS LYNCH

W. W. Norton & Company | *New York · London*

Copyright © 2010 by Thomas Lynch
First American Edition 2010

All rights reserved
Printed in the United States of America

For information about permission to reproduce selections from this book,
write to Permissions, W. W. Norton & Company, Inc., 500 Fifth Avenue,
New York, NY 10110

For information about special discounts for bulk purchases, please contact
W. W. Norton Special Sales at specialsales@wwnorton.com or 800-233-4830

Manufacturing by Courier Westford
Book design by Chris Welch
Production manager: Anna Oler

ISBN 978-0-393-04208-5

W. W. Norton & Company, Inc.
500 Fifth Avenue, New York, N.Y. 10110
www.wwnorton.com

W. W. Norton & Company Ltd.
Castle House, 75/76 Wells Street, London W1T 3QT

1 2 3 4 5 6 7 8 9 0

for Mary

CONTENTS

I

II

III

I

*Defraud not thyself of the good day, and let not the
part of a good gift overpass thee.*

—JESUS BEN SIRACH, 14:14

Euclid

What sort of morning was Euclid having
when he first considered parallel lines?
Or that business about how things equal
to the same thing are equal to each other?
Who's to know what the day has in it?
This morning Bert took it into his mind
to make a long bow out of Osage orange
and went on eBay to find the cow horns
from which to fashion the tips of the thing.
You better have something to pass the time,
he says, stirring his coffee, smiling.
And Murray is carving a model truck
from a block of walnut he found downstairs.
Whittling away he thinks of the years
he drove between Detroit and Buffalo
delivering parts for General Motors.
Might he have nursed theorems on lines and dots
or the properties of triangles or
the congruence of adjacent angles?
Or clearing customs at Niagara Falls,
arrived at some insight on wholes and parts
or an axiom involving radii
and the making of circles, how distance

from a center point can be both increased
endlessly and endlessly split—a mystery
whereby the local and the global share
the same vexations and geometry?
Possibly this is where God comes into it,
who breathed the common notion of coincidence
into the brain of that Alexandrian
over breakfast twenty-three centuries back,
who glimpsed for a moment that morning the sense
it all made: life, killing time, the elements,
the dots and lines and angles of connection—
an egg's shell opened with a spoon, the sun's
connivance with the moon's decline, Sophia
the maidservant pouring juice; everything,
everything coincides, the arc of memory,
her fine parabolas, the bend of a bow,
the curve of the earth, the turn in the road.

Montbretia

for Michael O'Connell

Montbretia blooming up the Moveen Road,
never native to the flora hereabouts,
arrived more than a hundred years ago
when sons of the Dutch-born landlord both went out
to fight for the crown in the Boer Wars.
One was killed. One came home with flowers—
this orangey iris from South Africa,
named for a botanist somewhere in France
who was named for the hill that he called home
a century before. It was ever thus—
from the place, a people; from the mass, particulars:
this tribe, this kind, this crowd, this sort, not that.
From all of time, this late July, this moment;
from every other one, this one and only.
Especially we name the wars and flowers,
the chieftains and discoverers, gods and lovers.
So: *Crocosmia, crocosmiiflora*
from the family *Iridaceae*—
those subdividing tongues and etymologies,
those lists and plots, old myths and litanies.
The seedling planted in the great-house garden
leapt the stone walls of the Vandeleurs
in the beak of a bird, on gardener's boot or breeze

and spread through Kilrush, round Poulnasherry
and out the townlands of the estuary,
all the way to Loop Head where West Clare ends,
and where some western in his anecdotage,
accounting for the rock off that peninsula—
that limestone tower, that god-awful keening—
fashioned a story of star-crossed lovers
who, running from love's grievous binding knot,
or striving for some distant privacy,
leapt the chasm to the tiny island.
One version holds they both leapt back again.
One made it and one fell to death, withal
we've named whatever perched or nested there:
storm petral, common tern and herring gull,
Dermot and his Grainne, Cuchulain and Mal,
shearwater, fulmer, *Larus argentatus.*
Thus, Loop Head is the place where lovers leapt
and found, like wars and flowers, everything
repeats itself—the setting out, the settling in,
the loop unwound winds up itself again;
the story, the screech of seabirds, the voice of gods,
in every leap some landing and some fall;
the seed, the stone: in every start an end.

Fr. Andrews

Jake, for the record, life does go on. Tuesday
gives way to Wednesday unremarkably.
The stars in their firmament behave like stars.
The morning traffic makes its mindless way
from one preoccupation to another.
Little changes. You knew as much yourself:
we have our day and others after us,
into their sparkling moment and out beyond.
We have our little say and then are silent.
But still, you met the mourners at the door,
and pressed the heavens with their lamentations
and tried to make some sense of all of it,
then saw them to the edge and home again—
the way we see you now, our level man,
out of the morning's worship into the sun,
the coach at the curb, and on your way again.

To Be Among These Elegant Voices

This image of the plump-faced peasantry
all knees and codpieces dancing round
someplace in Belgium at a wedding I found
among the *B*'s in *Artists—European*.
The way the book is printed, how it's bound
is a matter of indifference to me.
I want what's in it—the thousand words' worth
on every page—the contemplation
of its creator's life and times, the memory
of the moment I first beheld it
in Detroit, at the Institute of Arts
with that bookish girl I was trying to get,
as we used to say then, biblical with.
Was it 1970? Was it April?
Was she as lovely as I remember?
Was it "Yes, that's it, oh yes" she whispered?
Or have I confused her with another?
But wait—the place is full of echoes now.
Across the room among the *W*'s
in *English Romantic Poetry* Words-
worth is pacing out his iambic tune:
The child is Father of the Man . . .
his footfall sounding in the garden's gravel,

while Keats and Coleridge proceed uphill.
Or maybe it's that one word—"biblical"—
that sets us rummaging through the Scriptures.
Job, that long-suffering protagonist,
hapless, damaged, put upon by friends—
"Blessed be the name of the Lord," he yet insists
in that vexing, God-awful, answerless book.
It disturbed his people and disturbs us still.
"Sometimes," says Alan Dugan in a poem,
"Disturbed people go to the public library . . ."
He's right, of course, books can make us crazy,
or give us hope, or make us question things.
Where else but in our public library
can we indulge our curiosities,
imagination dancing in the round,
as one notion chases after others?
To be among these elegant voices
can get you going off in all directions
and get you back somehow from whence you came.
Take this place for example, all these choices:
Hobbies, Reference Books, Biography,
Fiction, Magazines, all these places, people, names
shelved and silenced alphabetically,

some dead and gone, still singing all the same.
Emily Dickinson, Mark Twain, James Joyce
whose Molly and Leopold, whose Huckleberry,
whose *After great pain a formal feeling comes*
become sweet fodder for our hungry minds,
or common guidance for our ruminations,
timely as the moments we occupy.
Today's the eighth of June. What else is new?
My wife and I are going to a wedding.
The world's supply of heartache is secure.
There's love and hate and mayhem everywhere.
We've come to dedicate some space to words,
some rooms for visions and remembrances.
It's good to look through windows on the world,
from a corner of a quiet place. Good
to keep the records and corrected texts,
histories and newspapers and ancient tracts
of what we human beings were doing here.
I was just browsing in *American Poets*
to find some good words for the nuptials—

some verse by which to toast the newlyweds—
when I came across this poem called "The Dance"
by William Carlos Williams. What it says
about the *tweedle of bagpipes,* about
a bugle and fiddles and *rollicking measures*
and *Breughel's great picture, The Kermess*
makes me grateful for the things we find in books:
this painting of peasants dancing in Flanders,
the poems on paintings and marriages;
the books they're in, the places where the books are kept.

Red

So you see, perspective is everything:
the angle, the frame, the way the light spills
into the moment, how the eye beholds
the thing that happens, out of everything.
Here's an example: you recall that thing
Doctor Williams wrote about the red wheel
barrow: how so much depends upon it?
There were other things—the glaze of rain water,
the white chickens. I never really got it
until my oldest boy's dog killed a cat—
a kitten only, it was my youngest boy's—
snapped its wee neck with a single shaking;
the way blood splattered on the garage wall,
red drops on the white boards. It wasn't raining.

Corpses Do Not Fret Their Coffin Boards

after Wordsworth

Corpses do not fret their coffin boards,
nor bodies wound in love their narrow beds:
size matters less to lovers and the dead
than to the lonely and the self-absorbed
for whom each passing moment is a chore
and space but vacancy: unholy dread
of what might happen or not happen next;
this dull predicament of less or more's
a never-balanced book, whereas for me,
the worth of words is something I can count
out easily, on fingertips—the sounds
they make, the sense, their coins and currencies—
these denouements doled out in tens, fourteens:
last reckonings tapped out on all accounts.

Libretto di Gianni Gibellini

When they bore the baker's son
out of Duomo di Modena
where he'd sung in the choir
with his father years before,
the bread of angels poured through the air
and a last ovation rose
over the white maple coffin
covered in sunflowers
all hailing the true body
of the beloved maestro,
while the throng in the piazza
stood silent beneath
the opening notes of
his famous aria:
no one shall sleep, no one shall sleep,
and all the nations mourned

the awful hush of *Il Tenore*.
All except one local priest,
Don Georgio Bellei, who claimed
it was "a profanation of the temple,"
to let that corpse in the cathedral—
a man, after all, who'd left his wife,
fathered a daughter out of wedlock,
and married a woman half his age.
The cleric's begrudgeries were
detailed in the evening paper.

It was Gianni Gibellini,
the *"um becchino"*
himself among the first to hear
that perfect instrument gone still,
who'd closed his mouth and closed his eyes,
dressed him in tails and white bow tie,
wound a rosary in one hand
and white kerchief in the other,
and laid him out in crimson velvet;
when he read what the priest said,

in the *Corriere della Serra,* swore:
"Porca miseria! That idiot priest
should keep his mouth sewn shut,"
then eased his hearse into forward gear
and processed slowly to Montale Rangone
on the outskirts of town,
humming Puccini on his way.

Oh Say Grim Death

*First minister of
Jaffrey Center 1782 -
1858
1757-1858   76 years
Jaffrey Center NH*

No doubt the Reverend Ainsworth read from Job
Over the charred corpse of the deacon's boy
To wit: "Blessed be the name of the Lord"
Or some such comfortless dose of holy writ
That winter morning after the house fire
Put all the First Congregationalists
Of Jaffrey Center, New Hampshire
Out weeping and gnashing, out in the snow
While the manse at Main Street and Gilmore Pond Road
Blazed into the early Thursday morning.
God's will is done as often without warning
As with one. Either way, *Revere His laws*
Is cut into the child's monument
To rhyme with a previous sentiment:
Cease, Man, to ask the hidden cause. As if
The answers ever were forthcoming. So
Little's known of young *Isaac A. Spofford*—
His father, *Eleazar,* his mother, *Mary,*
His death on the *thirteenth of February*
In *Seventeen Hundred Eighty-eight.*
A brand plucked from the ashes reads the stone
Of Rev. Laban Ainsworth's house; which frames
The sadness in the pastor's burning faith,

In God's vast purposes. As if the boy
Long buried here was killed to show how God
Makes all things work together toward some good.
And yet the stone's inquiry still haunts:
Oh say, grim death why thus destroy
The parents' hopes, their fondest joy—
Or say, instead, grim death destroys us all
By mighty nature's witless, random laws
Whereby old churchmen, children, everything—
All true believers, all who disbelieve,
Come to their ashen ends and life goes on.

Account

That year they kept the usual routines:
aubade and evensong; they watched the news,
worked house and grounds, paid taxes, alms and dues;
fed the animals, studied stars for signs,
ate right, slept soundly, hoist the cups half full,
counted their blessings, prayed for those at war
and strove, in all aspects, to be grateful,
earnest, discerning, even-tempered sorts.

Nonetheless they felt themselves forsaken
by God sometimes, sometimes by those they loved—
the ones who died, the ones who, not yet gone,
were grown distant or better left alone.

But Hark! For all their losses, all's restored
when Lo! Behold! To them a child is born.

Eleventh

It has to do with prayer and meditation—
seeking through them somehow to improve
contact with God, such as we've come to know Him.
Prayer's a thing I thought I understood:
Give me. Show me. Why me? Or else, *why not?*
The heavens were, for their part, unresponsive.

So, now I walk a bucket of oats and nuts
down to the beasts of burden in the field
and stand and watch them bowing to their meal,
grateful I suppose, though quiet's kept.
Such times as these I sense the silence is God-
willed: dumb welcome to my own mum thankfulness.

The Life of Fiction

Everything must, of course, advance the cause
of atmosphere or character or narrative:
the walk up the coast road, the sudden rain,
the stone shed at the sea's edge to shelter in,
the two of them waiting out the weather,
pressed into the corner, alone at last.
This is an old movie. It's Hollywood.
Each gets to tell the other everything—
old dreams and longings, slow regrets, how things
happen as they are supposed to happen,
or so they will console each other.
Of course, the usual embraces. They smile and weep.
They touch each other's faces wordlessly
then step out into the eventual sun,
each knowing what the other wanted known.
Or here's another possibility:
It doesn't rain. Or when it does,
a helpful pilgrim happens by and shouts,
"Hop in, you'll be perished, I'll get you home!"
And they get back safely, dry and comforted,
grateful for their dispensations. Life goes on.
The sea and the weather keep coming and going.

After Your Going

There was this hollow after your going
as if the air you'd lately occupied
having waited for you these long years sighed
at your leaving; as if the light were lonely
and the day bereft and the evening lost
without your habitation, and the room,
once you vacated it, returned to stone
and fire and a chair and the old ghosts.

Thirteen for Sean at Thirty

It was on this day in 1496
Da Vinci tried out his flying machine.
It failed; he crashed, but kept hard at it.
Helicopters, parachutes, ornithopters—
birdlike contraptions that fell to earth
as all must do, with thud and bruises.
God knows some days we all feel like losers.
The heart, it turns out, like a leaf in autumn,
like Leonardo, that 3rd of January,
between swoon and sure damage, rapture and doom,
never a stasis; and yet we fly, never for certain
if we're coming or going or whether we've gone
partway in the journey or partway home.

II

Rejoice greatly, O daughter of Zion; shout,
O daughter of Jerusalem: behold, thy King cometh
unto thee: he is just and having salvation; lowly, and
riding upon an ass, and upon a colt the foal of an ass.

—ZECHARIAH 9:9

Dear Mr. President

The black cow we put inside
for Mrs. Murray to inseminate
got its head stuck in the metal gate
and couldn't get it out.
What was she thinking
we said to each other.
Talk about a rock and a hard place.
Maybe it swelled some
after she forced it through.
Still, we couldn't get it out
though we kicked with our boots,
twisted it every which way,
cursed, swore, shouted, prayed.
Nothing worked.
The thing was stuck
and we were stuck with it.
How could we go back to our lives
with that beast out there,
its fat head caught in the gate?
We couldn't go to church
or the movies or the store.
What would we say when folks ask,
how are things? As they do.
In the end we had to get a saw—

one of those big round yokes
that makes an awful noise
and cuts through anything.
After everything we just cut it out—
it was that simple, Mr. President—
we just cut it out.
One clean cut at the corner,
bent it open until she pulled
her thick head out and stood there looking
like cows do, you know,
blameless, serviceable and dull,
just in time for the bull
which comes in a suitcase now,
says Mrs. Murray, the inseminator,
wearing a blue rubber glove
all the way up to her shoulder
pushing deep inside that beast,
all the while looking
up into the high roof joists of the shed
where swallows were nesting.
The look on her face—Mrs. Murray's—
was, I have to tell you, Mr. President,
so sublime, so beautiful.
We said there is a science to everything.

Local Heroes

Some days the worst that can happen happens.
The sky falls or evil overwhelms or
the world as we have come to know it turns
towards the eventual apocalypse
long predicted in all the holy books—
the end-times of old grudge and grievances
that bring us each to our oblivions.
Still, maybe this is not the end at all,
nor even the beginning of the end.
Rather, one more in a long list of sorrows
to be added to the ones thus far endured,
through what we have come to call our history—
another in that bitter litany
that we will, if we survive it, have survived.
God help us who must live through this, alive
to the terror and open wounds: the heart
torn, shaken faith, the violent, vengeful soul,
the nerve exposed, the broken body so
mingled with its breaking that it's lost forever.
Lord send us, in our peril, local heroes.
Someone to listen, someone to watch, someone
to search and wait and keep the careful count
of the dead and missing, the dead and gone

but not forgotten. Some days all that can be done
is to salvage one sadness from the mass
of sadnesses, to bear one body home,
to lay the dead out among their people,
organize the flowers and casseroles,
write the obits, meet the mourners at the door,
drive the dark procession down through town,
toll the bell, dig the hole, tend the pyre.
It's what we do. The daylong news is dire—
full of true believers and politicos,
bold talk of holy war and photo ops.
But here, brave men and women pick the pieces up.
They serve the living, caring for the dead.
Here the distant battle is waged in homes.
Like politics, all funerals are local.

Dear Mr. Vice President

It was one cow trying to
mount the other—
"bulling" they call it hereabouts,
though in fairness
the bull was nowhere to be found—
just one black and white cow
with a pink udder
and its own agenda
trying to mount another,
for reasons unknown to your
humble correspondent,
that fractured the latter's hindquarters
so it lay out in the high meadow,
looking oafish and put-upon.
It couldn't move or graze,
couldn't make its way to water.
It made for itself an awful noise—
that low-grade plaint
cows make while calving,
but worse somehow: a hopeless case.
Squinting upland through his window
J.J. could make out something wrong.
He tractored it down into the
haggard to tend to it, bringing it

fresh grass, sups of water, carrying on
the mindless conversations
humans have with larger mammals.
For days it just lay there
shitting itself, making its lament,
J.J. hoping it might find its way
back into the brutish world
nature had assigned to it.
He spoke to the priest
and lit a candle. He called the vet
who came and had a look.
But it was broken. That was obvious.
It was going nowhere.
He sent for Coffey then
who came with his truck
rigged with a crane and length of cable.
After putting a kill shot
between its eyes, Coffey hoisted it
into the grey evening air.
That moment it hung there in the sky,
Mr. Vice President,
the deadweight mass of its disaster,
its limbs akimbo,
the glaze of its eyes,

its bestial ruination pure,
the misery it was so
suddenly out of—
all of it put me in mind
of the charred corpses
of those men they strung
from the bridge that time
after dragging them
through the mob and town—
that silhouette of broken parts
twisted by gravity and damage
into misdirection.
"Ah hell," J.J. said,
"it's entirely fucked."
Disconsolate,
Mr. Vice President,
that is the word
that came into my brain
when J.J. said
"ah hell," again,
and again, "it's fucked."
Then went inside
and closed his door
to everything out there
where he had been.

Himself

He'll have been the last of his kind here then.
The flagstones, dry-stone walls, the slumping thatch,
out-offices and cow cabins, the patch
of haggard he sowed spuds and onions in—
all of it a century out of fashion—
all giving way to the quiet rising damp
of hush and vacancy once he is gone.
Those long contemplations at the fire, cats
curling at the door, the dog's lame waltzing,
the kettle, the candle and the lamp—
all still, all quenched, all darkened—
the votives and rosaries and novenas,
the pope and Kennedy and Sacred Heart,
the bucket, the basket, the latch and lock,
the tractor that took him into town and back
for the pension cheque and messages and pub,
the chair, the bedstead and the chamber pot,
everything will amount to nothing much.
Everything will slowly disappear.
And some grandniece, a sister's daughter's daughter,
one blue August in ten or fifteen years
will marry well and will inherit it:

the cottage ruins, the brown abandoned land.
They'll come to see it in a hired car.
The kindly Liverpudlian she's wed,
in concert with a local auctioneer,
will post a sign to offer *Site for Sale*.
The acres that he labored in will merge
with a neighbor's growing pasturage
and all the decades of him will begin to blur,
easing, as the far fields of his holding did,
up the hill, over the cliff, into the sea.

Dear Madam Secretary

It was the bucket of oats
I was giving the mare ass
that gave her wee she-foal the shits—
out there in the haggard
gazing at the wall
incomprehensibly,
the green ooze
staining her rear flanks,
her entire aspect badly shaken.
Milk scours—P.J. diagnosed it—
and sent me to Williams,
the chemist in town,
for a big syringe
and some sort of dose
to restore the poor creature's
proper fettle.
It was pink—the dose was—
and it smelled like berries.
Mornings and evenings
we'd bring her inside,
and get her to
suckle a finger or thumb
then plunge the medicine

down her throat.
In no time she was
out gamboling in the
sweet grass, pulling at
the pink dugs of the mare ass,
good, we figured, for donkey's years.
Not so the painful case
of a weanling Friesian
that got a chill
from the cold rain
of a late June night—
out in the low field,
down and wheezing.
Pneumonia, we figured
and could only hope
the injection we gave it
would save the thing.
I found it in the shed
the following morning,
dead as any specimen
has ever been.
And what I wanted
to share with you, Madam Secretary,

out there with the shovel,
digging the grave,
is that husbandry
has its disappointments.
What I am trying to say
is that the way of things
will not be tampered with.
Or, as one of your
colleagues once opined,
"stuff happens."
Surely what he meant to say
was shit, Madam Secretary.
It's shit that happens.
Ask any ass.

That March

Early Easter.
Across the Mid-
west there was snow,
floods of rain and
in the news more
"grim milestones":
dead and wounded,
that same brown war
we'd waged since March
Two Thousand Three
and what is worse,
the same grinning
ignominy,
joking, dancing,
carrying on
as if nothing
mattered. As if
nothing was wrong.
Neither the dead
nor the damaged,
the litany
of woe and toll:
to currency,

economy,
the poor planet,
the armed forces,
the price of oil.
Not to worry—
he kept saying—
go to the mall.
Spend some money.
Not to worry—
he kept saying—
I'm almost gone.

Dear Messrs. Attorneys General

It's living on the cliff road
makes it easy—what's done
with surplus kittens hereabouts
or yelping collies once
the bitch has whelped,
involving a sack, a rock,
the cover of nightfall
or early morning.
Times like these,
as you know yourselves,
Messrs. Gonzales and Mukasey,
require such extremes.
Here on the frontlines
it's all we can manage,
any day, any one of us,
to handle the dispatches.
And if the ends do not
justify the means, still,
ends are what we're after. Nonetheless,
there's something to behold—
May I call you Alberto?
May I call you Michael?—
Something wondrous in the

rendition of the thing:
the kicking bundle swung into oblivion,
the arc of its descent,
the great gulp of the ocean over it,
the cleanly disappearance, not a trace,
not a quibble, not a corpse;
everything, even the memory of it,
swept away in the wind and tide.
The Prevention of Cruelty crowd
have the law on their side, lads.
But we have orders.

The Names of Donkeys

Truth told I got the first one for the lawn—
to keep the haggards shorn. An idyllic
notion—nature taking care of nature,
naturally—a daft Arcadian's
nature-ignorance. Still, it's a farming townland.
Grass is fodder here. The yearlong traffic
is in pasturage—round bales, heaps and silage—
feed is everything. "Where there's dung there's money,"
P.J. Roche once said, mucking out the cabins
where he kept his cows all winter, before
he built that massive slatted house
that lets the slurry ooze through spaces in the floor
into a tank that's emptied twice a year.
"There's fierce growth and greening in it." So,
it wouldn't do to have a little mower.
This patch of West Clare's not a city lot,
or subdivision parcel. Not at all!
This cottage is my people's first freehold,
a shelter fashioned out of thatch and stone,
against the rising damp, god-awful elements.
That's the ocean noising over those high fields.
The pike's Mouth of the Shannon's just a walk.
On this peninsula we are surrounded.
Grass and ground are holy. Thus, the donkey.

Of course, I called it "Charles" from the start,
after the prince. I couldn't help myself.
I love a little dagger of contempt
tucked in the warm cloak of celebration,
in every deference an intimation
of darker purposes or metaphor.
In Charlie's case it was the ears, of course,
the piebald prepossession, its upright bearing,
that bonnie, if at times buffoonish look
as if it knew how ridiculous it is—
the planet, the humans, the other animals—
we're all pretending, always falling short,
always aspiring to something that we're not:
I felt a kinship with him, like a brother,
driven by selfsame hungers and desires,
creatures of the parable and paradox,
agreeable at times, at times contrarians,
our own worst enemies, our only friends.
I'd watch him at his duties in the yard
gobbling the greensward and geography,
shitting, sleeping, staring at a wall,
content by all appearances, serene,
bearing his crosses, keeping his own counsel,
much as I figured I myself was doing.

It took a while before he'd let me touch him.
The bucket of oats, the sup of water,
the dumbly standing by while he was at it—
these were the tools by which I gained his trust.
In his own time he'd let me brush him
and take the nipper to his growth of hooves.
One day for sport P.J. Roche was up and on him,
grabbing on his mane, his legs tucked round him,
racing down the field. He was so fast!
We knew we'd chance him in the local derbies
and made his racing name "The Moveen Lad."
He ran in Cross and Doonbeg and Kilkee
and finished in the money every time
although the first-place cup eluded him.
In Carrigaholt, we thought he took the prize,
but the Garde, Charlie Killeen, said John McMahon's
breedy Spanish ass won by a nose.
It was more than he could manage, I suppose:
to have his donkey namesake win the day.
"I call them as I see them," is what he said.
"Same as ourselves," I told him, smiling.
Then into Morrisey's for pints around,
figuring and refiguring accounts—
we make out Charlie got it either way.

It was the braying, that unholy yawp—
it would wake the sleeping neighbors and the dead—
so full of primal vocatives. I thought
some vexation's left him crazed and overwrought
and wondered what it was until I spied
that length of mighty throbbing member. "Christ!"
I said to myself. "I see now. Yes, of course,"
and promised that I'd find some consort for him.
I watched the want ads in the *Champion*,
the *Farmers Journal* and the *Buy & Sell*.
I went to fairs in Ennis and Kilrush,
I asked around, I made a couple calls.
"Surely by Christmas," I told him. But no such luck.
All winter that mad-anxious roaring rose
out of the old cow-cabins P.J. turned
into three fine stable stalls and stable yard.
We built a huge corral for training horses—
a syndicate we called "Roche's Stables,"
because P.J. had that gift bred in the bone,
and I—a here-today-and-gone-tomorrow Yank—
wanted shelter for himself when I was gone.
That April in the *Champion* we saw:
"Fine piebald donkey, filly, two years old."
We quibbled at the cost but brought her home.

And when I first clapped eyes on her I saw
what Michael Morgan meant when he said "fine"
because she was—so fetching, a small, lithe
fish among thick animals—well worth her price.
And to see them, Charles and Camilla,
as, you will forgive, I could not help but call her,
because those nuptials were in the news,
that and the pontiff's death and funeral,
but to see them, together in the yard,
the gratitude and rapture in his eyes,
her reticence at first and then the signs
by which she signaled she would not refuse him.
"Mighty nature" P.J. Roche once called it—
the mystery by which two separate things
become one thing to make, somehow, another.
And there it was, not quite the full year later,
one morning there in miniature, a creature
out in the haggard, shining and piebald,
with its mother's ears, the body of a hare,
shivering, suckling, standing upright there,
as if the lesser beasts made up its retinue.
It had this oafish, overeager look,
a little swagger and a boyish grin,
and so I called him George, George W.

Word got round about my stallion Charles,
"The Moveen Lad" was whispered in the pubs:
a rocket racer, a willing sire, a blood
line certain to be the stuff of legends.
We got a call from Sinon Flanagan
who'd four mare asses and no able jack.
Might I consider sending Charlie back
to spend a month in service to his harem?
What male thing wouldn't rise to such occasions?
I'd often fantasized the very thing.
What harm, I thought, the more the merrier.
But I was wrong. Poor Charles came back wrecked.
His kindly gratitude turned brutish lust.
The former tenderness gone bollocks mad,
he'd hunt all other male things from the shed
and chase the ponies round the stable yard
biting at their fetlocks, manes and private parts
and could not be trusted round the calves and cows.
We locked him up in solitary hold,
like shuffling captives at Guantánamo,
thinking the confinement would restore his calm.
But when he worsened, with regrets, we settled on
castration as the only way to go.
Where more's the pity, less is sometimes more.

Before that remedy old Charles spent
one late midsummer evening with Camilla.
A last hurrah, a second honeymoon,
their old romance rekindled in the dark—
whatever happened, something surely sparked
because before the solstice, that following June,
behold, a snow white she-ass foal appeared
beneath the hedgerow where Camilla sheltered.
By which time Charles, lately gelded, was
no less the head case than he'd been before—
more daft than ever and a little sore—
so, for his own sake, re-incarcerated.
We bring him oats and nuts, a sup of hay—
and pray he has forgiven what's been done,
and let him out to roam between good gates.
Sometimes we race him and sometimes he wins.
Whereas for George, George W., what an ass!
Feckless and unrepentant, as if he knew
his kind bore saviors through Jerusalem
or gravid virgin-girls to Bethlehem.
Witless as a tin of tuna, craven, crass,
donkey stubborn, donkey stupid, dull as soap,
for all his epic bloodline, little hope.
We've put him up for sale but no one calls.

We call the little she-ass Sarah P.,
though truth be told we had some choices.
When it comes to names and asses, there's no shortage.
With foals-at-foot the future's up for grabs.
So, fools-at-heart or honest brokers,
much the same as with our sons and daughters,
good naming doesn't shape the outcomes, still
we nurse our little dreams and leave the rest
to whoever is in charge here: who's to know?
Fate? Chance? God in His heaven? I don't know.
All we can hope for is for time to tell—
another day, another season, donkey's years
to undo some the mess we've made of it,
to make amends, to make some small repairs,
reset the table, rearrange the chairs,
to let the ones we love know that we love them
and let the others know we bear them no
especial malice, then leave well enough alone.
And sometimes when I am out among them
in the evening, when all the work is done,
I think I hear the voices of those gone
before, who stood this ground in their own times,
and bore their burdens—great and small alike—
and all they ever say is carry on.

III

If they ask you, "What is the evidence of your Father in you?" say to them, "It is motion and rest."

—GOSPEL OF THOMAS 50:3

Walking Papers

to Michael Heffernan

I reckoned reading Frost would put you right
and making something from a line of his
a better way to use what's left of time
than trying to diagnose what's killing you—
something your doctor said about something
he gathered from something in your latest labs,
letting slip some quibble about blood work
or enzymes or liver function. Listen—
something's going to get you in the end.
The numbers are fairly convincing on this,
hovering, as they do, around a hundred
percent. We die. And more's the pity.
Same for the goose as for the gander, true
for both saints and sinners, fit and fat.
We get our dose of days and after that
we get whatever is or isn't next:
heaven, remembered, a kick in the ass,
a place in a frame on some grandkid's piano,
a grave, a tomb, the fire, our ashes scattered,
the scavenging birds, the deep, nirvana—
sure, one oblivion's good as another.
By all accounts there's nothing to it, pal—
a cakewalk, kicked bucket, falling off a log;

one moment you are and next you aren't,
the way that semicolon slipped in there
before the comma in the following line
three lines before the coming period.
You can think of it as punctuation
and maybe take some comfort from that, friend—
a question mark or exclamation point—
no matter, we're all sentenced to an end,
the movers and the shakers, bons vivants,
all ne'er-do-wells and nincompoops, savants,
sage and sluggard, deft and daft alike:
everyone's given their walking papers.
Everyone's shown the door and sees the light.
The adverbials are incidental,
dull as any devil in the details
and though the eulogists are reverential
once it's over no one gives a wrap
whether tumor, tantrum, stroke or heart attack,
too many cigarettes, too-frenzied sex,
too many cheeseburgers, too old an age,
a murderous shellfish or tsunami swept
the creature from creation's little stage,
waving and smiling, kicking and screaming,

at ease or agonizing, anyway,
the hush, the breathlessness, it's all the same.
The month, the day, the year, the proper names,
the size of the stone, what gets cut in it—
I had a lovers' quarrel with the world.
Enough's enough. Good riddance. Less is more.
I told you that I wasn't feeling good!
Together wing to wing and oar to oar—
but footnotes to insuperable truth:
we mortals come with our mortalities,
freighted, laden, born with our last breath in us.
Why worry whether this or that improves
or ruins your chances. No guarantees
come with our particular models—we
get our final markdowns, deep discounts:
a coupon good for something more or nothingness.
So quit the medicos and pharmacists,
who've got a pill for whatever ails you—
restless leg or ornery bowel,
a lapsed erection, cauliflower ears,
sugar, tapeworm, loose stools, septicemia—
I say clean your plate and say your prayers,
go out for a long walk after supper

and listen for the voice that sounds like you
talking to yourself, you know the one:
contrapuntal, measured to footfall, true
to your own metabolism. Listen—
inspiration, expiration, it's all the same,
the sigh of creation and its ceasing—
whatever's going to happen's going to happen.
Who knows the number when your number's up?
So, go on out and count some syllables,
lay some lines down one after another,
check the pulses, make the meters tick,
make up whatever noise you have to make
to make some sense of the day that's in it.
I have my doubts on almost everything.
I sit in church and think these hooligans
are only fellow pilgrims, like myself,
no more beatific than a heap of bones,
lost and grinning for no apparent reason.
That said, I've had these glimpses, inklings,
sometimes it's almost as if I'm haunted.
Things come to me as apparitions do.
My late father, for instance, my dear mother,
just now that fellow Frost you like to quote,

they often reappear in lines like these
as if they had a message meant for me
which echoes with a thing I've always known:
Life goes on. Forever. It's impossible.
Remember when it cost just fourteen cents
to send a sonnet on an index card?
"The postal service imitating art"—
which one of us said that, my lettered friend?
And now we carry on page after page
as if we both depended on it still.
We carry on and pay the going rate
because we keep as articles of faith
there might be something for us in the mail.
God knows we could turn up, the two of us,
long after our long correspondence goes
silent as all such correspondents must.
Maybe someone will get some wind of us
in some old book or in the bonfire,
the firebug rising to its occasion,
the way the frost appears then disappears,
a door that swings both ways on its hinges . . .
It could happen. We could go on forever.
If so we'll want a code word, secret sign,

something to make it known we recognize
each other. How about "New Hampshire"?
How 'bout we grab our groins or give a wave,
like third-base coaches when the count is full,
to signal *take a pitch* or *guard the plate,*
go for the walk or *runner stealing home*?
To signal all is well, we're not alone,
we'll both of us turn over in our graves.

Argyle's Stone

Around his neck Argyle wore a stone:
green marble from the strand at Iona
where Columcille and his banished tribesmen
landed after bloody Cooldrevny claimed
three thousand lives in 561 A.D.
"To every cow its calf; to books their copy!"—
that civil notion begat the savagery.
His ruminations on such histories
put him in mind of how most mortals kept
committing the same sin over and over
like calving cows or Psalter manuscripts—
each a version of the original.
Among his pendant stone's known properties:
general healing, protection from fire,
shipwreck, miscarriage and other dire
possibilities that might imperil
a pilgrim of Argyle's appetites.
Foremost among the sin-eater's lapses
were hunger, which was constant, and then thirst,
and all known iterations of desire—
craving and coveting, lusting and glut:
whatever was was never quite enough.
So, for ballast among such gravities
Argyle wore the stone for anchorage.

Shelling

Darling, I bring you these
oddments from a far shoreline.
They have borne the deep and shallow,
light and dark,
earth and air and sea,
some living things, some dead,
some things yet to be.
And now, here,
precious among the elements,
my love, your gaze.

Epithalamium

That man who was married in the same black suit
he was laid out in, years later, and buried,
his widow's tears—they might all make sense to you,
now that the two of you are to be married.

You've seen old photos of the two of them
taken seven decades back or more.
They showed up smiling and said, of course
we will, for better or for worse, and then

they raised their glasses, cut the cake and kissed
and tossed the bride's bouquet and garter out
and thanked their parents and assembled guests,
then danced until the candles were blown out,

then danced some more; they were that enamored.
And who could blame them, so nearly perfect
in their flesh and finery and desires;
in all ways poised and blessed and elect

as you are now, and may you always be:
each of you eager to please the other,
to let the selfish minute pass, to see
yourselves perfected always in each other.

That old man, when he was young, he brought his bride
home to the house he had readied for her,
and swept her up and carried her inside
as was the custom then, and then together

they helped each other out of their new clothes:
his gabardines, her lace and satin gown,
his tie, her veil, his buttons and her bows
then stood there looking at themselves, alone.

Before they fell into their embracing,
because they thought they'd need them in the end,
they tucked their garments carefully away
in cedar boxes underneath the bed.

And when the going got a little rough
when patience frayed or tempers flared, when love
seemed to have left them only filled with loss
as in all lifelong marriages it must,

when forgiveness and forgetting seemed
impossible, they'd kneel beside their bed
and bury their faces in those wedding things—
her tears, his curses, her fears, his pride and dread,

all dried and muffled in that day's old raiments
which smelled of their sweet youth and promises.
And though they never settled everything,
they did their best to do the next best thing.

Argyle at Loop Head

Argyle kept to the outposts and edges,
cliff rocks, coastal roads, estuary banks,
sheltering in dry ditches, thick hedges,
forts and cabin ruins, beside stone ranks,
much scorned by men, much put-upon by weather.
The weeping of keeners brought him hither,
fresh grief, fresh graves, lights in dark localities—
such signs and wonders of mortality
drew him towards the living and the dead
to foment pardon in a bowl of beer
or leaven remission out of common bread,
and when his feast was finished, disappear.
The bodies of the dead he dined over
never troubled Argyle but still
their souls went with him into exile
and, reincarnate as gulls and plovers,
dove from high headlands over the ocean
in fits of hopeful flight, much as heaven
was said to require a leap of faith
into the fathomless and unbeknownst.
Sometimes the urge to follow them was so
near overwhelming he could almost taste
the loss of gravity in brackish air,
his leap, the sea's embrace, his savior.

Calling

We Catholic boys all listened for The Call.
The Voice of God, exquisite in our ears—
Come follow me, or, as it was with Paul,
Thunder, enlightening, the bang and whisper
By which God makes His will known to us all.
Be fruitful. But not apples. Is that clear?

Or as it was with Noah, *Build an ark.*
Or Abram, *Prove your faith, man, kill your boy.*
Or Moses, *So you're thirsty? Smite the rock.*
Or Job, out of the whirlwind, *Gird your loins.*
Or that fervent girl-child, Joan of Arc,
Who burned but never renounced her "voices."

Belief is easy when God speaks to us.
The ordinary silence—there's the thing—
The soul-consuming quiet, the heavens' hush
That sets even the pious wondering.
Lord spare us all, we doubting Thomases,
Who, even with a trembling finger in

The wound, still ask aloud, "My Lord? My God?"
Ever curious, too inquisitive.
I was named after a "Fr. Tom"—
My father's uncle, Thomas Patrick Lynch,
A sickly boy who died before his time,
(1904–1936)

Saving Apaches at Rancho de Taos
Breathing some easier that rarified air
Of the Sangre de Cristo Mountains.
The blood of Christ, when he was done, ran clear.
Once in the basement of my grandparents' house
I found his cassock and Roman collar

Hanging from a rafter, blessed and bodiless
And under it, a trunk of priestly things,
Surplice and biretta, bright chalices,
A sick call kit and leather breviary.
I tried them all. Though nothing seemed to fit,
All the same, I kept on listening.

And I served at altar for our parish priest,
The Reverend Thomas Kenny—never "Tom,"
Never wavering, never doubtful in the least—
A Holy Roman Irish Catholic man
Who lost his bearings when they Englished everything,
Like Barry Fitzgerald or Fr. Flanagan.

After morning Masses, he'd make me kneel
For half an hour in the back of church
To offer thanksgiving for the holy meal
I was after having in the Eucharist.
"Be stingy with the Lord, boyo, and he'll
Be stingy in return." He kept a list

Of saints and shortcomings, shalts and shalt-nots,
Mortal, venial, deadly, and cardinal sins,
Contrary virtues, graces, gifts of God,
The glorious and sorrowful mysteries,
Holy days, first Fridays, stations of the Cross,
Corporal and spiritual works of mercy.

It was a language I learned to speak,
Lovely and Latin, a sort of second tongue—
My parents' and people's, the nuns' and priests'—
That rose in the air like incense and song
Ghostly and Gregorian, like memories:
First gushing, then going, but never gone.

And I am listening, listening still.
"We're given two ears and one mouth for good reason.
Pray to know God's purpose and you will."
So said the old priest, and I believed him.
"*Carpe momentum,* boy—each minute is a gift."
And though I wonder still, sometimes I seize it.

Sometimes I see that dead priest in my dreams
In the basement of Desnoyer's Funeral Home
In Jackson, Michigan—he's on the table.
The train has brought him home from Santa Fe.
Two men in shirtsleeves vest and casket him
While my father, just gone twelve, stands in the door

Unnoticed, watching, watching everything.
Upstairs his father's organizing things—
The flowers, Mass and burial, a stone.
The fifth of August 1936:
That Wednesday morning when our dad was "called"—
Or so he always told us after that—

To this life's work between the quick and dead.
And so we do, these generations since,
My brothers, sisters, sons and daughter, all
Carry on as if we'd heard it too—
That silence or that summons—who's to know
Whether faith moves mountains or if mountains move?

Argyle's Eucharist

Upright over corpses it occurred to him—
the body outstretched on a pair of planks,
the measly loaf and stingy goblet,
the gobsmacked locals, their begrudging thanks,
the kinswomen rummaging for coppers—
it came into his brain like candlelight:
his lot in life like priesthood after all.
Such consolations as the kind he proffered,
by sup and gulp consuming mortals' sins,
quenching hellfire, dousing purgatory,
transforming requiems to baptismals;
but for holy orders and a church,
bells and vestments and lectionary,
a bishop, benefice or sinecure,
the miracles were more or less the same:
a transubstantiation, sleight and feint,
a reconfiguration of accounts
whereby he took unto himself the woe
that ought betide the rotting decadent.
Perdition due the recent decedent
thus averted by Argyle's hunger,
the unencumbered soul makes safe to God,
the decomposing dead get buried under
earth and stone. The sin-eater belches, wipes his gob.

Asleep

Often as not I crawl in bed like this,
wondering if the general discontent,
the ball and socket misery, sore ass,
shortness of breath, the tightening sense
of doom and occlusion close at hand,
might mean the dark is nearer than the light
and death's dull angel, like a one-man band,
is warming up to play my tune tonight.
I think of my sons and how they'll find me
a little purple on the side I sleep on,
still warm (*postmortem caloricity*),
some rigor in my limbs. My wife weeps on
cue as they roll in the gurney. They take
me out feet first, downstairs, next door for a wake.

On a Bar of Chinese Soap

The way the bee and flower on this bar
of Chinese soap will suds into a blur
of common form and purpose is not far
from how in due course memory obscures
the edges of what happened and what didn't.
In time it's all befuddlement: names, dates,
loves, hates, what in fact was said, what wasn't.
And thus this slow immersion compensates,
this laving of the body and the mind,
this anointing by both bee and flower
from which we're left at length to rise, alive,
cleansed, buzzing and fragrant, free of the dire
consequence of time, the dour habits
of the heart, the sore flesh it so inhabits.

Alchemy

for Mike & Marilyn Kinna

After everything it's like the tune
we keep humming over and over
mostly for how it makes us remember
somewhere back in our shimmering youths,
before the household and the furniture,
before the children and the mortgage and the pets;
back when it was only the two of us,
only each other to abide, obey,
suffer and satisfy, endure, survive;
only one another to have and hold
and that hush that would sometimes settle between us,
and the light—how it turned silver in the dark,
till everything we touched turned into gold.
In time we came to know that tune by heart.

Lament

In memory of Robert Foley, 1927–1999

You always said I'd get you in the end—
the joke long-standing between us, Foley—
as if the twenty years you had on me
guaranteed you an earlier heaven.
We'd grin and get back to our local jobs—
your civic duties, my slow processions.
You always had a head for numbers, Bob,
and could be counted on to keep accounts of things:
how principals and interests get amortized,
when enough's enough, the lives and times
of ancestors, the birthdays of grandchildren,
Lenten observances, the rites of spring.
So here we are, your priest, your townspeople,
your brothers and sisters and their families,
your sons and daughters and their sons and daughters
your beloved Virginia, all here, gathered round
to these grave duties. We give you back to God
a little grudgingly. We want to keep
your easy laughter, your fierce protections,
your honor and your loyalty and graces.
Still, even in the ground we see reflections:
the image of your hope in these men's faces,
your love in their sisters', your faith in their mother.
Good husband, father, brother, kinsman, friend—
you got it right—in the end, we get each other.

A Corporal Work of Mercy

"God bless all here, the living and the dead!"
Thus spake Argyle ducking through the door.
A woman's corpse outstretched on the stone floor
was yellow jaundiced and so corpulent
the wizened man hunched sobbing next to it
in deep paroxysms of grief and shame
could neither hoist her on the table nor
drag the fat cadaver from the place.
So setting candles at her head and feet
he'd kept the vigil raising his lament
whilst praying for sufficient aid to move her
before he was evicted by the stench.
Argyle, moved by such entreaties, bent
such powers as he had to the removal,
taking up those huge shanks by the ankles
he hauled away and the husband pushed her.
After half a morning's massive labors
they'd got her out the back door to the haggard—
a heap among the spuds and cabbages
of putrefaction and composting grief—
and knowing that the job was incomplete
they set to work with spades and dug a ditch
of such surpassing depth and length and breadth . . .
it was after dark they shoved her into it.

Monaghan's Fish Market

He liked to look at cases full of fish
filleted and laid out like the swarm of souls
on the Sistine Chapel ceiling Michelangelo
painted for the pope. Sometimes a whiff
of the ocean rose off it as he passed
or possibly the fishmonger's daughter,
that bright-faced girl, maybe it was her
who smelled of the sea and the tide ceaselessly
coming and going and the thick damp grass
of the headlands and the blue air's incensing.

Refusing at Fifty-two to Write Sonnets

It came to him that he could nearly count
How many Octobers he had left to him
In increments of ten or, say, eleven
Thus: sixty-three, seventy-four, eighty-five.
He couldn't see himself at ninety-six—
Humanity's advances notwithstanding
In health care, self-help, or New Age regimens—
What with his habits and family history,
The end he thought is nearer than you think.

The future, thus confined to its contingencies,
The present moment opens like a gift:
The balding month, the grey week, the blue morning,
The hour's routine, the minute's passing glance—
All seem like godsends now. And what to make of this?
At the end the word that comes to him is Thanks.

ACKNOWLEDGMENTS

The author is grateful to the editors of the following journals where these poems first appeared.

The Atlantic Monthly: "Fr. Andrews"
Commonweal: "Euclid," "Shelling," "Alchemy," "Lament," "Eleventh"
Dunes Review: "Himself"
The MacGuffin: "That March," "Monaghan's Fish Market," "Corpses Do Not Fret Their Coffin Boards"
Michigan Quarterly Review: "Local Heroes," "To Be Among These Elegant Voices," "Walking Papers"
Muse (Madonna University): "Argyle's Stone," "A Corporal Work of Mercy"
The Poetry Center of Chicago Broadsides: "Refusing at Fifty-two to Write Sonnets"
Poetry Ireland Review: "Montbretia," "The Life of Fiction," "On a Bar of Chinese Soap"

The Poetry Review (London): "Red," "Dear Mr. President," "Epithalamium"

Seneca Review: "Dear Mr. Vice President"

The Southern Review: "Argyle at Loop Head," "Argyle's Eucharist"

Stand: "Asleep," "Dear Madam Secretary," "Dear Messrs. Attorneys General"

Stinging Fly (Dublin): "The Names of Donkeys," "After Your Going"

U.S. Catholic: "Calling"

Willow Springs: "Libretto di Gianni Gibellini"

"Oh Say Grim Death" was commissioned by Evan Chambers for his orchestral suite *The Old Burying Ground* and read in performances at the Kerrytown Concert House, Hill Auditorium and Carnegie Hall.

"Montbretia" appears in the anthology *Three-Legged Stool: Voices of Clare,* edited by Brian Mooney and Arthur Watson, FX Press.

"To Be Among These Elegant Voices" was published in a limited-edition broadside to mark the opening of Highland Township Library, Michigan.

The author is likewise grateful to Jill Bialosky, Robin Robertson, Richard McDonough, Michael Heffernan, Matthew Sweeney, Richard Tillinghast, Keith Taylor, Dennis O'Driscoll, Philip Casey and Mary Tata, each of whom has shaped the poems collected here.